SEND THE RIGHT MESSAGE

A Writing Handbook

by Dan Tricarico
Tricarico Consulting
www.tricaricoconsulting.com
tricaricoconsulting@gmail.com
(858) 699-8615

WELCOME!

Tricarico Consulting is a communication achievement service specializing in improving writing skills in the small business arena.

To help you with your small business writing needs, Tricarico Consulting offers:

- This handbook
- Employee presentations and workshops
- Writing for hire. Call me for a quote!

We wish you the best with your small business communication needs.

Phone: (858) 699-8615

Email: tricaricoconsulting@gmail.com

Tricarico Consulting (858) 699-8615

TABLE OF CONTENTS

Introduction....................	**Page 4**
Structure......................	**Page 7**
Sentences	**Page 25**
Paragraphs.....................	**Page 36**
Vocabulary.....................	**Page 41**
Punctuation....................	**Page 45**
Revision.......................	**Page 53**
Business Correspondence..........	**Page 60**
Conclusion.....................	**Page 71**
Resources......................	**Page 72**
Acknowledgments................	**Page 74**

INTRODUCTION

"Fill your paper with the breathings of your heart."
~William Wordsworth

In the James Brooks' comedy *Broadcast News*, the character played by Albert Brooks is on the phone with his news producer. The woman, played by Holly Hunter, also happens to be his friend. At one point, Brooks' character says, "Let's go to that place by that thing where we went that one time," and the joke is that, having been friends for so long, she understands exactly what he means.

In writing for business, however, we do not have the same assurance that our audience will comprehend our meaning. Therefore, as writers, there are a couple key elements we must refine so that we develop the confidence that our readers will follow our message. We want our writing to be fluent, confident, and persuasive, while still maintaining our individual writer's voice and style, as a writer's voice and style are as distinctive and individual as fingerprints.

For years, I've been telling my students that if they learn nothing else before they walk out of my workshops they should make sure they learn the two most important elements of good writing: precision and clarity.

PRECISION

Precision refers to the idea of saying exactly what you mean. This is largely due to vocabulary. That's not to say that it's important to sound smart or knowledgeable or to use the biggest word in the dictionary. What's important is to use the *right* word that communicates the *specific* message you are trying to send. In fact, long or hard to understand words can interfere with our message, confusing or frustrating our readers. In our attempts to sound intelligent, we often alienate our audience. Consequently, each word you learn is a tool in your writer's toolbox, and so the more words you know (and can use accurately and effectively), the more successful you will be as a writer.

CLARITY

Clarity, on the other hand, refers to making your message as clear as it can possibly be. This is achieved largely through having a logical structure for your overall piece of writing, as well as for each individual sentence. It also means organizing your thoughts in a way that creates a progression of ideas that is clear to the reader. Furthermore, clarity is a function of sentence structure, accurate punctuation, and a well-written and specific point. Once again, trying to impress readers with overly written or flowery prose will just annoy them and, since most of your writing will be read by peers, customers, or supervisors, annoying your audience could have decidedly negative effects.

As a thoughtful practitioner of clarity and precision, you can minimize the consequences of inferior writing. Whether you're composing your doctoral dissertation or penning a note to hang on the fridge saying you went to the 7-11 for a cherry Slurpee, employing precision and clarity will increase your chances of communicating your message effectively and, as a result, getting what you want.

And isn't that what communication is all about?

STRUCTURE

Just as a building without proper architecture and constructed with a flawed foundation will ultimately collapse as a result of its own imperfection, a piece of writing that is not properly structured will crumble in on itself and fail both its reader and its writer.

Structure does not have to be complicated, however. First, make certain your writing possesses a distinct beginning, middle, and end. Secondly, state a clear, controlling point (often called the "thesis" or "claim."). Finally, include specific and relevant details to clarify that point. These strategies will ensure that every component is where it should be and that your message is effective, easily understood, and clearly communicated.

Here are some common elements of structure to keep in mind when you write:

STEPS IN THE WRITING PROCESS
1. Pre-writing
2. Rough Draft
3. Peer Response/Self-evaluation

4. Revision
5. Final Draft

Pre-writing. The first step in the writing process is to plan. If you were to take a road trip to Michigan, you wouldn't just jump in the car and go because chances are you would get lost or you would waste too much gas trying to find your way. The same is true with writing. Without a "road map," you will get lost.

Rough Draft. The first draft is about getting down all the information. Stephen King calls it the "All Story" draft. Just get it down. Don't worry yet about spelling, grammar, and punctuation. This is where you want to be lost in the heat of composition.

Peer Response/Self-evaluation. A funny thing happens when you look at a piece of your own writing. Your mind, already certain of what you meant to say, will correct the mistakes that appear on the page as you read—*automatically.* Like magic.

So handing it to other readers and asking, "Does this sound all right?" is critical. Since they aren't in your mind and don't know what you intended to say, they will see every misspelling, every omitted word, every formatting problem, and every passage that bores or confuses the reader. If I give a piece of writing to my peers and ask for feedback and they hand it back unmarked, saying, "That was pretty good," I'm disappointed. Without feedback, I don't know what works and what doesn't, what is vague or unclear, or how effective the piece is overall. In short, I don't know what to fix.

Revision. This is the most important step in the writing process. This is the step where you take what you have and make it better. Adopting a critical eye, your mission is now to polish the overall structure, search out and fix every spelling, grammar, and punctuation error, and rewrite muddy or bumpy parts for clarity. Repeat this step until the piece of writing is as sharp and sculpted as you can make it.

Final Draft. This is where your writing puts on its power business suit, picks up its briefcase, and goes to work. After polishing your piece of writing, you must adhere to any guidelines that accompany the type of writing you're doing, and submit a nice, neat, professional-looking final draft. This will almost exclusively result in a typed copy. Typing standards typically include double-spaced copy, 12 pt. font (10 pt. is too small and 14 pt. is too big) and no odd or strange fonts. The typeface should look like writing in a printed book. Many writers use Times New Roman exclusively when they write.

SECTIONS OF EXPOSITORY WRITING
1. Introduction
2. Claim (see below)
3. Topic Sentence
4. Example
5. Analysis
6. Conclusion

Introduction. The introduction of your piece of writing has three major objectives: 1) Gain the reader's attention, 2) Introduce your topic, and 3) State your claim or thesis.

Claim. The Claim (also known as the Major Thesis) is the overall point you are trying to make and is typically broken up into two parts: subject and opinion (or value judgment).

Sample Claim: Television shows are too violent.

Subject: Television shows
Opinion: Are too violent.

Topic Sentence. If your writing has multiple paragraphs or sections in the body of the piece, each paragraph should probably begin with a topic sentence. Topic sentences are mini-thesis sentences that also have subject and opinion and tell the reader what *that* particular section or paragraph will be about.

Example. As with arguments you have with a friend, co-worker, or spouse, specific examples strengthen your position and can result in the resolution you desire. In the case of your writing, examples can be specific details in other literature (books, reports, pamphlets, etc.), empirical data and statistics, and personal or anecdotal examples. The key is to choose the example that is the strongest support for your particular main point. Using several strong examples only strengthens your position.

Analysis. Analysis is the author's interpretation, insight, commentary, and opinion about the example and why the claim is important. If you are taking a stand in your writing, and you've given proper support with strong examples, you will spend a great deal of the writing discussing your stand and why it is valid.

Conclusion. Each piece of good writing needs an ending. Your conclusion should begin by restating (not repeating) your main point (the claim) and wrapping up all of your ideas. There is no room in the conclusion for new information or ideas and, additionally, it should contain all commentary and analysis, meaning that this is not the place for new facts or statistics.

Reference Page/Works Cited Page. In a paper where you cite information from other sources, it is imperative that you say where you got that information. There is a specific format for listing such information and the two organizations that govern such formats are

The Modern Language Association (MLA) and the American Psychological Association (APA). See the Resource page at end of book for more information.

AUDIENCE, PURPOSE, TONE, AND CLAIM

Before you ever put pen to paper or fingers to keyboard, you should make some initial decisions in terms of audience, purpose, tone, and claim.

Audience. Whenever you communicate a message to someone, it's very important to know your audience. The funny stories you tell your friends at the Happy Hour, for example, might be very different than the funny stories you tell your co-leader at Vacation Bible School or the ones you tell your grandmother over turkey, mashed potatoes, and cranberry sauce at Thanksgiving.

Before composing a single word, ask yourself: Who is my audience? For whom am I writing? Sometimes it even helps to imagine a "perfect reader," someone who is a good listener, is eager for your message, and is interested in your success.

Considering your tone will help you make choices in terms of format, structure, tone, and word choice.

Purpose. Every piece of writing must have a purpose. In other words, there must be some *reason* you've decided to write the piece you're writing. There are as many purposes as there are types of writing. Purposes include to inform, to entertain, to instruct, to remediate, to explain, etc. Knowing why you are writing something can save you time, trouble, and energy by focusing your efforts in the right direction from the beginning.

Tone. Tone is the emotional vibe that a piece of writing gives off when a reader reads it. It involves the feelings that the reader gets when reading the piece as well as the feelings authors convey through their word choice, sentence structure, and organization. Should your piece have a more formal tone? Informal tone? Should it be light-hearted and comical? Serious? Remorseful? Business-like? Personal? Once you decide on the tone, or emotional stance you wish to convey, then you can determine what to write and how to write it.

Claim. Every piece of writing should have a claim. In the old days, the writer's "claim" went by other names such as main idea, major thesis, or controlling purpose. Before you write, it's important to know what your main idea is and what message it is that you're trying to communicate. The claim may or may not appear explicitly in the piece of writing; it is sometimes an implied claim, meaning that by the time the reader finishes your piece, they should be able to paraphrase your main point.

As stated before, the claim usually has two parts: subject and opinion. The subject is what the writer is writing about (novel, poem, article, issue, self, etc.) and the opinion is what the writer is trying to say or prove about the subject. The claim is then supported throughout the rest of the writing with supporting examples and analysis/discussion.

Here is another example of a claim:

Sales numbers can improve if we diversify our sales team to cover different areas of the city.

Subject: Sales numbers
Opinion: can improve if we diversify our sales team to cover different areas of the city.

Notice how the opinion is debatable (i.e., others might disagree) because the writer has set up an argument that he or she will prove in the remainder of the piece. Key opinion words ("improve"/"diversify") allow the writer to riff off of specific ideas in the analysis and discussion sections.

PATTERNS OF ORGANIZATION

One of the decisions a writer must make is what kind of organization or structure the piece of writing should take.

Some of the most common structures are:

1. Description
2. Sequence
3. Cause and Effect
4. Problem and Solution
5. Comparison and Contrast
6. Topic

Description. In this method, the writer uses factual information and sensory imagery (word pictures that appeal to the five senses—

sight, sound, taste, touch, smell) to convey the message to the reader. Whether it is a description of an object, place, or person, using descriptive imagery can be an effective method of communication. The writer can describe such elements as size, shape, physical specifications, dimensions, or characteristics to create word pictures that the reader can envision which will aid in understanding.

Chronological Order/Sequence. A very logical organizational method, using sequence simply means that as you write, you are listing things in order in which they occur. First this happened, then this happened, and after that, this happened, etc. Obviously, this method works well, then, for writing about things that occur in a certain order or sequence or follow a logical progression.

Cause and Effect. A somewhat more complex structure, cause and effect organization relies on an understanding of what the stimuli are (which would be outlined first) and then what is happening that is a direct result of that stimuli.

Problem/Solution: Similar to cause and effect, the problem/solution structure is two-fold: First, the writer outlines the problem and, secondly, communicates any solution that he or she feels might help. This is a particularly good structure for a business letter or memo, for example.

Comparison/Contrast: When a writer needs to compare and/or contrast two concepts, characters, events, or people, a comparison/contrast structure might work best. In this model, the writer typically compares the various elements first (discusses how they are similar) and then contrasts them (discusses how they are different).

Topic. A final way to organize your thoughts is by topic. For example, if you are writing about several different characters in novels, you might organize your essay to discuss different aspects of those characters by topic: social standing, moral development, motivation, etc. By dividing the writing by topic, the writer helps the reader more easily follow the flow of ideas.

PLAGIARISM

Presenting any information that has come from another source as your own is called plagiarism. Essentially, it's stealing. The best way to avoid looking as if you are plagiarizing material is to clearly cite the sources you used to get your information.

In the field of research writing, there are two basic methods for documenting sources: MLA or APA. The Modern Language Association (MLA) is an organization that decides how research papers should look and consequently dictates form, such as documentation of sources. The American Psychological Association (APA) has also developed a format for research, due in part to the number of people completing master's thesis papers and doctoral dissertations in the field of psychology.

RHETORICAL APPEALS

The rhetorical appeals refer to what methods of persuasion a writer uses in a piece of expository text. The three main rhetorical appeals are ethos, pathos, and logos.

- ***Ethos***. The rhetorical appeal of ethos has to do with using authority, ethics, or expert testimony to make your point. This may include quotes from experts, your credibility due to your credentials, or any other approach that relies on the use of authority to persuade the reader to believe in the author's claim.
- ***Pathos***. This approach deals with emotions. Think of the words sympathy, empathy, and pathetic. This is where a writer, usually through word choice and detail, appeals to the reader's emotions.
- ***Logos***. Statistics, studies, data, and logic are what drive the rhetorical appeal of logos. This is for writers and readers who rely on the credibility of facts and data to be persuasive.

STRUCTURE TASKS

Here are some practice tasks that will help you consider how to plan and structure your writing

A. PRACTICING PRE-WRITING

Pre-writing is a critical step in the writing process that many lazy writers skip. Put yourself ahead of the game by finding a planning/pre-writing method that works for you.

If you are a more spatial thinker, consider using a mindmapping/webbing approach, or if you are a more linear/sequential thinker, try using an outline, columns, or brainstorm/listing approach.

The important part is NOT to skip this step.

Practice some pre-writing methods below:

B. PRACTICING CLAIMS

Claims have two parts: subject and opinion. Write a claim for each of the following areas, as it pertains to your business: 1) Sales, 2) Marketing, 3) Inventory.

    A. Sales Claim:

    B. Marketing Claim:

    C. Inventory Claim:

C. PRACTICING YOUR "HOOK"

List three ways you can gain your reader's attention—often called a "hook"--and write a short introduction paragraph for a memo, email, or report.

A.

B.

C.

Write practice introduction paragraph here:

D. PRACTICING SUPPORTING EVIDENCE

Again, choosing from the following topics (Sales, Marketing, Inventory) write one piece of FACTUAL supporting evidence you could use in a memo or report about your business. REMEMBER: The supporting evidence MUST be factual (measurable and provable):

A.

B.

C.

SENTENCES

The sentence is the most basic individual unit of writing. It is the job of every individual sentence to communicate information as well as to work together with the other sentences to help create an overall rhythm to the paragraph. Sentences, therefore, should be clear and complete to effectively communicate and they should vary in length and type to add an interesting dynamic to the overall piece of writing.

Below are some of the most basic elements of sentence construction:

SENTENCES
1. subject/predicate
2. subject/verb agreement
3. phrases
4. independent clauses
5. dependent clauses
6. noun/pronoun agreement
7. modifiers
8. run-ons/fragments
9. modifiers
10. parallelism
11. tense
12. capitalization

13. numerals
14. specific nouns/strong verbs

Subject/Predicate. Every sentence has two parts: a subject and a predicate. The subject is the noun part—the who or what that is doing the action. The predicate contains the verb, or the "action" part, the "what" that's being done. If you are missing either part, you end up with what's called a fragment, which is just a piece of a sentence. While fragments can sometimes be used effectively for impact, it is not recommended in business writing because along with run-on sentences, they can make it look as if you cannot control your sentence structure.

Phrases. A phrase is a group of related words that function as a unit of speech. However, a phrase lacks a subject and/or predicate or both, so it cannot be considered a complete sentence.

Subject/Verb agreement. A verb must agree in number with its subject. You wouldn't ever write, "The supervisors is on vacation." The noun (supervisors) is plural, so the verb has to plural (It should be "are" or "were," not "is" or "was"). This is easy enough to determine, but when sentences get more complicated it is necessary to make sure that the subjects and verbs agree in number. It also pays to keep in mind that subject openers like "neither," "either," "each," "every," and "everyone" are singular and so require singular verbs (as in "Neither Mark nor DeAnna is going to the Winter Formal." Even though Mark and DeAnna sound like the subject, the subject is—technically speaking—the word "Neither," which is singular.).

Independent Clauses. An independent clause is a short sentence that contains a subject and verb and expresses a complete thought. Example: *Steve walked.* "Steve" is the subject and "walked" is the verb. Since it also expresses a complete thought, it can be considered a complete sentence.

Dependent Clauses. A dependent clause (also known as a subordinate clause) contains a subject and verb as well, but since it begins with a subordinating conjunction, it cannot stand on its own and express a complete thought. Common subordinating conjunctions include *after, before, because, until, whenever, where, and wherever.*

Example: *Before we attend the sales conference in June.* "We" is the subject and "attends" is the verb, but since it begins with the subordinating conjunction "Before," it renders the clause incomplete and unable to stand on its own.

Other examples might include: *After contacting our clients. Until we decrease our overhead. Since we are diversifying our product line.* Dependent clauses rely on, or are "dependent" on, independent clauses to make sense. Example*: Before we can assess our new direction, we must look at the data.* The use of dependent clause generally results in a more interesting and mature use of sentence structure.

Noun/Pronoun agreement. All pronouns must agree in number, person, and gender (sex) with the noun they refer to (known as the "antecedent"). Example: *Sheila* brought *her* laptop to the conference. This gets tricky with multiple people and multiple genders. Consider sentences like "Is either Travis or Belinda allowed to bring his or her reports to the meeting?"

Modifiers. A modifier is a phrase that gives more information about another part of the sentence, usually the noun or verb. Scour your sentences for misplaced and dangling modifiers which often create unintentionally humorous sentence construction.

Example: Eating the donut, my nose was covered in frosting.
My nose doesn't eat donuts, so this is a misplaced modifier. What comes at the beginning of the sentence must modify the subject of the sentence (in this case, the first noun following the comma). So in this case, you would want an independent clause beginning with who was actually eating the donut.

Parallelism. Parallelism is the practice of repeating similar grammatical structures to give writing rhythm. Typically, this means making sure all elements are in the same part of speech.

Wrong: Chris enjoys running, working out, and to go swimming.
Right: Chris enjoys running, working out, and swimming.

Tense. Depending on the purpose of the piece of writing, you will need to decide if you should write in the present tense ("Our sales numbers *are* improving") or the past tense ("Our sales number improved last November"). The most important aspect of tense is not to shift tenses midway through the piece of writing.

Capitalization. Proper capitalization has become a challenge in a world where communication is short and swift due to texting, e-mail, and social networks (which often restrict the number of characters allowed), causing people to cut corners. But proper writing requires proper capitalization.

Numerals. Generally speaking, numbers from one to nine are usually written as words; numbers 10 and over are written in numerals. Exceptions, however, include when the number is used at the beginning of a sentence and for the uses of very large numbers where a combination may be used (1.5 billion, 25 million, etc.).

Specific Nouns/Strong Verbs. When constructing sentences, using specific nouns and strong verbs can add clarity and power to your message.

Instead of saying "fruit," say "apple," and instead of that say "the Golden Delicious apple with the wormhole in it." The more specific the noun, the more information you are able to give your reader. Strong verbs, on the other hand, help give your message action and movement. Instead of saying "The man walked slowly up the street," try to keep in mind that there might be one word that means the same thing as "walked slowly." Try something like "The man strolled." The stronger action is clearer and gives muscle to your sentence.

SENTENCES TASKS

Here are some practice tasks to help your construct sentences concise, powerful, and graceful sentences.

A. Write ten sentences using parallel structure (where each part of the sentence is grammatically symmetrical)

1.

2.

3.

4.

5.

6.

7.

8.

9.

10.

B. The following sentence is vague and uninteresting. Rewrite the example sentence using specific nouns, strong verbs, and clear images.

Example Sentence: The fruit fell from the tree.

Rewrite a new version (using specific nouns, strong verbs, and clear images) here (try several, in fact):

C. By circling F for FACT and O for OPINION, label the following ten sentences as either FACT or OPINION.

1. The first Stars Wars movie was the best.
    F   O

2. Humans first walked on the moon in July, 1969.
    F   O

3. Our sales teams has increased sales 40% in the first quarter.
    F   O

4. Our sales team uses innovative and creative techniques to sell.
    F   O

5. I drank coffee with my breakfast this morning.
    F   O

6. Brad Pitt is hotter than George Clooney.
    F   O

7. Brad Pitt was one of the stars in *Oceans 11*.
    F   O

8. Dogs are easier to take care of than cats.
    F   O

9. The iPhone 6 is more aesthetical pleasing than the Samsung Galaxy.
    F   O

10. The iPhone has a single "Home" button to control its functions.
    F   O

Answers: 1) O, 2) F, 3) F, 4) O, 5) F, 6) O, 7) F, 8) O, 9) O, 10) F

PARAGRAPHS

Imagine that your paragraphs are like multi-colored Legos that you will use to construct your edifice. They are the building blocks of writing. First of all, however, you must decide what your edifice should look like—am I building an office building, a campsite, or a castle? Depending on the design of the overall structure, your blocks will vary in color, shape, and size.

According to the *Little, Brown Handbook*, the uses of a paragraph include:

- To introduce a main point
- To develop a key example or important evidence
- To shift approaches
- To mark movement in a sequence
- To transition to dialogue
- To introduce a conclusion in an essay

Here are some common concerns you should keep in mind when composing paragraphs in your business writing:

1. Topic
2. Topic Sentence
3. Unity
4. Coherence
5. White Space
6. Topic Sentence
7. Fact/Opinion

Topic. Every paragraph is a single unit of writing that should revolve around a single idea or subject. The paragraph should almost always begin with a topic sentence (see below). Each paragraph should function as a single brick in the overall architecture of the piece of writing.

Topic Sentence. The topic sentence is the sentence that tells what the main idea of the paragraph is. As stated earlier in this handbook, topic sentences typically have two parts: subject and opinion. There should be a subject that the paragraph will discuss and what the writer's opinion is of that subject—at least as far as that paragraph is concerned.

Unity. When each paragraph revolves around a single idea successfully, this is referred to as unity. Just as each paragraph should be a single brick in the architecture of the piece of writing, each sentence should be a single link in the construction of the overall paragraph. No sentence should be allowed to remain in the paragraph that doesn't support the overall main idea that particular paragraph, as well as the overall claim of the piece of writing. It kills the unity, for example, if a piece of writing that involves your trip to the Grand Canyon suddenly has a paragraph about when you went to Disneyland. The same is true for individual paragraphs that have a sentence or two that are off topic.

Coherence. As stated in the introduction of this book, clarity is one of the hallmarks of great writing. If you're not being clear, you will—without a doubt—compromise the effectiveness of your message. Each sentence should be written as clearly as possible and communicate your message. This is referred to as coherence. Coherence means that there is a logical expression of ideas and that they flow in a way that is clear to the reader. The difference between unity (mentioned above) and coherence is that unity means everything is on-topic (unified), while coherence means that each part is written as clearly as possible and flows logically. One method for ensuring coherence is to have another person read your writing and mark where the passages become muddy, vague, too general, or in any other way, unclear.

White Space. The term "white space" refers to the denseness of text on a page. The more solid blocks of writing on a page, the less white space. White space gives the reader's mind a break. Without enough white space, it will seem like an insurmountable chore to slog through long blocks of dense text. If your readers perceive (from an abundance of white space on the page) that your piece of writing will be an easy read, you have a better chance of reaching your audience and communicating your message.

Fact/Opinion. One of the most important distinctions in expository (informational) writing is being able to tell the difference between fact and opinion. Many people, though, have trouble telling the difference. To further complicate the matter, good writers often present their opinions so gracefully that they sound like fact. Skilled writers—not to mention skilled readers—know the difference between fact and opinion.

A fact is something that is measurable or provable. A football field is either 100 yards or it is not. You can prove it with a tape measure. Facts are important because they can be used to support claims and arguments. They lend credence to your points that persuade the reader to see things your way.

Opinion, on the other hand, is debatable. It is the author's take or perspective on a certain subject and someone else may feel differently. Opinion can also be called analysis, judgment, interpretation, evaluation, reflection, commentary, or ideas. Opinion provides depth, point-of-view, and perspective. Analysis often includes value judgments and superlatives--*good, better, best*--or personal opinion or feeling words.

VOCABULARY

"Never use a phrase when a word will do."
--George Orwell

Words are the individual tools of the writer. In the same way that a carpenter must know how to use a hammer, a saw, and a screwdriver, a writer must know how to use a noun, a verb, and an adjective. Writers must also have a thorough understanding of the difference between the dictionary definition of a word (denotation) and the emotional associations that word might conjure in the mind of the reader (connotation). Professional writers also work very diligently to choose words that communicate precisely what they mean.

In terms of vocabulary, however, the goal is not to use the largest word you can find. Instead, you should want to find the word that best communicates the message you intend to send.

Using the wrong word or the right word incorrectly can result in inadvertent messages. As Mark Twain once said, "The difference between the right word and the almost right word is the difference between 'lightning' and 'the lightning bug'."

Here are some elements to consider when choosing and working with individual words in your writing:

VOCBULARY
1. Tone
2. Denotation/Connotation (the emotional "tag" on a word)
3. misspelled/misused words
4. avoid jargon/sexist language

Tone. Tone refers to the feelings and/or emotional associations that permeate your writing. Generally, it is a function of word choice. The specific words you chose (and their specific denotations and connotations) can determine whether your tone is formal, informal, happy, sad, regretful, nostalgic, academic, forceful, or calm.

Denotation. Denotation refers to the actual, literal dictionary definition of a word. Two words may have the same denotation, but have wildly different connotations.

Connotation. Connotation refers to the emotional connections associated with a word or what one teacher use to call "the emotion tag." The words "cheap" and "inexpensive," for example, have the same dictionary definition or denotation (not costing a lot of money), but "cheap" has a negative connotation of not costing a lot of money because of its low quality, while inexpensive has the positive connotation of being a bargain or a good deal. When writing, then, it pays to consider both the literal definitions of words (denotation) as well as the emotional associations they possess (connotation).

Avoid jargon/sexist language.

Jargon. Every industry has its own internal terminology that only the participants in that industry generally understand. This terminology is known as jargon. Doctors, mechanics, scrapbookers, baseball players, insurance agents, car dealers, and butchers may all have words that are specific to their areas of expertise. In the interest of clarity, then, avoid filling your writing with jargon that can confuse a reader who may not be familiar with that business.

Sexist language. Sexist language needlessly distinguishes between men and women in such matters as occupation, ability, behavior, temperament, and maturity. Non-sexist language is more inclusive and can reach more people, whereas using sexist language in your writing can bother certain members of your audience in a way that alienates readers and interferes with the effective communication of your message. In revising for sexist language, therefore, a word like "mankind" becomes "humanity" or, simply, "people."

Sexist: Department Chairman (the unspoken implication here is that only a male employee can hold this position.)

Non-sexist: Department Chair or Department Chairperson (This implies that a person of either gender may hold this position.)

PUNCTUATION

Punctuation marks assist the reader in navigating a piece of writing. In essence, they are the road signs of writing. Like these signs, they tell when to stop (periods, question marks, and exclamation points), when to pause (commas and semi-colons), and where to turn (dashes, hyphens, and apostrophes).

If you saw no signs on the road as you drove to work in the morning, you would most likely see drivers wandering aimlessly, unsure of their purpose or destination, or in the worst case scenario, crashing into each other, unsure of who was doing what or who was going where.

Without proper punctuation, it's not cars but sentences and ideas that smash into each other, leaving frustrated and disoriented readers in their wake. It may seem small or picky, but even a misplaced comma can negatively affect your message.

Consider, for example, the difference in these two messages:

Let's eat, Grandma!

Let's eat Grandma!

The omission of one small squiggle mark on the page and suddenly we're cannibals. Proper punctuation saves lives!

Here are some of the most common punctuation marks and their uses:

COMMON PUNCTUATION MARKS
1. Commas
2. Colon
3. Semi-colon
4. Dash
5. Hyphen
6. Apostrophe
7. Quotation Marks
8. Ellipsis

Commas. There are many uses for the comma including separating items in a list or series, after an introductory word group, between two adjectives where "and" makes sense, connecting two sentences with a coordinating conjunction, and in dates, addresses, titles, and numbers.

Colon. The colon is most often used to call attention to the words that follow it, especially when those words form a list or series. *Example: The office work includes: typing, filing, and duplicating.*

It can also be used to add more information to an independent clause (short sentence). *Example: The solution is clear: we must hire more employees and give them all substantial raises.* In business letters, it is also used after the salutation. *Example: Dear Pat Smith:*

Semi-colon. The semi-colon is used to connect significant components of a sentence that are equal in value. It can be used between short sentences that are thematically related. *Example: Our approach was to increase the number of salespeople in the field; our attempts were successful.* It can also be used between two short sentences with a transitional element. *Example: Many businesses are going thriving in this booming economy; in fact, six new companies have opened so far this month.* It is also used in a series where there are already commas. *Example: Classic action movies include* Die Hard, *with Bruce Willis;* Rambo, *with Sylvester Stallone; and* Commando, *with Arnold Schwarzzenger.*

Dash. The dash is used to set off parenthetical material. *Example: Everything you're doing right—marketing, selling, and promoting—*

can still be improved. It can also be used to prepare a list. *Example: Our customer service goals are simple—commitment, convenience, and compassion.* Warning: unnecessary dashes can create a choppy effect that interferes with your message.

Hyphen. The hyphen is most often used between a two-word adjective. *Example: The second-hand couch fit nicely in our living room.* It is also used to avoid confusion between similar words such as *recreation* and *re-creation.*

Apostrophe. Use apostrophes: 1) to show possession (Mary's donuts. Plural and possessive? Try: The Storm Troopers' rifles didn't shoot well.); 2) to indicate an omission of a letter or letters, as in contractions (don't, can't, etc.); and 3) to indicate plural written items that are atypical of English language conventions (e.g., How many t's are there in "kitten?"). There are other uses, but these are three main functions of the apostrophe.

Quotation Marks. Quotation marks are most often used to set off direct quotations said by people. They are also used to set off long quotations of text. They are also used to punctuate shorts works such as the titles of poems, short stories, songs, and magazine articles. Sometimes quotation marks are used to set off words that are being emphasized. *Example: I'm not sure how much "training" he was actually doing.*

Ellipsis. The ellipsis mark consists of three spaced periods. It is often just called "dot, dot, dot." It is used to indicate that you have deleted words from another text (in essence, it is telling your reader, "I'm quoting from another source and there was other stuff here, but I took it out."). The ellipsis may also be used to indicate a hesitation or an interruption in speech or to suggest an unfinished thought. *Example: We expected there to be a downward spiral in the use of the iPhone, but. . .*

PUNCTUATION TASKS

A. Commonly Misspelled or Confused Words

When it comes to commonly misspelled words or confused words, there are certain errors that a successful business person simply cannot afford to make. Most of these have to do with words that sound alike (homonyms). It is critical that you understand the difference between words like too, to, and two; there, their, and they're; and the difference between affect and effect.

Complete the following exercises by circling the proper answer to check your knowledge of these commonly confused words:

1. In the morning, we are going (to, two, too) Aunt Jane's house.
2. I can't believe the way that movie (affected, effected) me emotionally.
3. We need to meet them at the station because (they're, their, there) coming in on the 9 o'clock train.
4. I don't think that looks like (you're, your) coat.

5. I like vanilla ice cream, but I like chocolate ice cream (to, too, two).

6. (There, Their, They're) is a place in Austin where you can hear the best Blues music.

7. (There, They're, Their) are (to, too, two) answers to your question.

8. I don't know what (your, you're) going to do, but I'm leaving!

9. I don't think that was the (affect, effect) you were going for.

10. Why do you always throw the dice off the table when it's (you're, your) turn?

Answers:

1) *to*
2) *affected*
3) *they're*
4) *your*
5) *too*
6) *there*
7) *there/two*
8) *you're*
9) *effect*
10) *your*

B. Write three sentences connecting two independent clauses with a semi-colon.

1.

2.

3.

C. Write three sentences that use a dash correctly.

1.

2.

3.

REVISION

In the movie *Finding Forrester*, Sean Connery plays a reclusive, Salinger-esque writer who tells his young writing apprentice that writers "write the first draft with [their] heart, but write the second draft with [their] head." The point here is that the first draft should be the passionate outpouring of all your ideas in the heat-of-the-moment composition and that this is not the time, generally speaking, stop to work out issues of spelling, grammar, and punctuation. Next, after giving that draft some time to cool (depending on your deadlines), you can go back to that piece of writing and attack the piece with a cooler, more critical eye, identifying and fixing not only the mechanics errors, but issues of overall structure and even formatting (typing, font size, margins, graphics, desktop publishing options, etc.)

Revision is one of the most important steps in the writing process because you're taking what you have and you're making it better. The word "revision," if you really scrutinize it, breaks down into two parts. The prefix "re-," means "again" and the word "vision," means "to see" or "to look at."

Technically speaking, then, revision means taking your writing and "seeing" it from a fresh perspective or "looking" at it "again."

ELEMENTS OF REVISION
1. Peer Response
2. Self-evaluation
3. Global Revisions
4. Line Editing
5. The Deadly Sins

Peer Response. A Peer Response is when you give your piece of writing to a peer, supervisor, or professional editor for feedback. Having a second pair of eyes review your writing is very important because they will almost certainly unearth misspellings, grammar errors, and vague or unclear passages you've missed.

Self-evaluation. A self-evaluation refers to you reviewing your own piece of writing, often in regard to a checklist or rubric that asks you to look for common errors.

Global Revisions. Global revisions are those changes that have to do with the entire manuscript. These include major overhauls to the overall structure (introduction, body, conclusion), the topic, or the purpose. It generally involves cutting or rearranging several paragraphs or major sections.

Line Editing. Unlike global editing, line editing puts each line of the manuscript under a microscope. You pull out each sentence, each line, and often each individual word and make sure that each small unit of writing is doing its job and pulling its weight.

A Final Note on Revision: The Deadly Sins.

It bears repeating that The Deadly Sins in business writing are sentence fragments, run-on sentences, subject/verb agreement issues, and incorrect capitalization. These four transgressions will make writers look as if they are not in control of their writing style and that can give the reader an inaccurate perception of the writer's overall intelligence. Always do whatever you can to ensure that you have eliminated these most basic of errors from each piece of writing you compose. The revision step of the writing process is the last chance you'll have to eliminate these errors and send out the most professional piece of writing possible.

Tricarico Consulting (858) 699-8615

REVISION TASKS

A. What are three questions you can ask yourself in a self-evaluation to improve your piece of writing?

1.

2.

3.

B. What are three parts of the piece you can evaluate in a GLOBAL revision to see if large-scale structural changes are necessary?

1.

2.

3.

C. List The Deadly Sins of poor writing.

1.

2.

3.

4.

BUSINESS CORRESPONDENCE

There are many types of business correspondence, and as with all writing, content should dictate form. Decide first what you want to say (Request for information? Complaint? Proposal? Report on data?), and then decide on the best vehicle for that message (business letter, report, memorandum, resume, e-mail, etc.). If you decide on the form first, you might find yourself cramming all your information into an ill-fitting container, which can feel a lot like going to a wedding in your bathing suit.

The most common modes of business correspondence include:

1. Business Letters
2. Memos
3. Resumes
4. Reports
5. E-mails
6. PowerPoint presentations
7. Press Releases

Business/Cover Letters. A business letter is a formal letter using established conventions and format to address issues in your business. A business letter includes a date, inside address, salutation, body, close, and signature. As Diana Hacker says in *Rules for Writers* (6th edition), "In writing a business letter, be direct, clear, and courteous, but do not hesitate to be firm if necessary." State your purpose early on and include only the most pertinent information. Remember business breaks down to mean "busi-ness" and many people are too busy to read long letters. Cover letters are essentially business letters that are used to "cover" another type of document or package—a resume, perhaps, or a report or other type of submission.

Memos. Short for memorandum and often contained within a particular business or organization (typically called "inter-office memos"), memos are usually concise and either report information, make a request, or recommend an action. Always follow the established conventions and formatting of memos, depending on your industry standards.

Resumes. Faced with stacks of resumes, human resource personnel often don't spend very much time looking at each resume, so your format must be clear, to the point, easy to read, and pleasing to the eye. While listing all of your relevant background and experience, resumes are typical limited to a page or two and organize your experience by category (Objective, Education, Professional Experience, Awards and Achievements, and References, etc.). In today's digital world, most resumes are submitted electronically.

Reports. Reports are fully-researched papers or proposals that typically deal with the results of research, action plans, or changes in policy. They can be lengthy and are often presented in folders, binders, or other attractive packaging. Usually reports are divided into sections and each section serves a specific purpose including summaries, statements of intent, problems, solutions, and conclusions. When you prepare a report, be certain that you are following the established format for the type of report you're producing, research thoroughly, consider your audience, and revise for clarity.

E-mails. Many business people find their in-boxes jammed with e-mails every day, from very important messages about their job to the cutsie "chain" e-mail with inspirational quotes and/or pictures of adorable kittens. Show people you value their time and format your e-mail following established conventions and keep your message to the point. Always include a relevant description of the message in the "Subject" line, put the most important part of the message in the beginning of the message, keep paragraphs short, and use the same punctuation and grammar rules you would follow in a business letter (avoid texting "shorthand" and uncapitalized letters which can come off as unprofessional).

PowerPoint Presentations. Although not technically restricted entirely to writing, Power Point presentations can be an important mode of business communication that often relies on the effective communication of text. Power Point presentations use a series of organized slides to explore an idea, teach a concept, or cover a topic. These presentations are made with the PowerPoint computer program and, as the speaker gives the presentation, the slides are typically projected on a large screen for an entire room to see. *Warning: Do not fill your slides with text and simply stand there reading to your audience. This will bore them and will NOT send the right message!*

Press Releases. A press release is a written document intended to announce a newsworthy item. Typically, it consists of what journalists call The 5 Ws and the H (Who, What, When, Where, Why, and How). Typically, the releases are sent to newspapers and magazines, as well as radio television stations. Press releases follow a specific format—they are short, factual, and to the point, yet they convey the company's enthusiasm for the new item, product, or event. As a general rule, press releases are written in paragraph form and are almost never more than a single page.

BUSINESS CORRESPONDENCE TASKS

A. When drafting a memo, you must know what your point is (claim), who it is intended for (audience), and how you want it to sound (tone).

After answering those questions below, please draft a practice memorandum:

What is your claim?

Who is the memo intended for?

What kind of tone should it have (Friendly? Thoughtful? Serious? Admonishing?)?

Draft your practice memo here:

B. Choosing either Sales, Marketing, or Inventory as a topic, structure a 10-15 slide Power Point present that you will give to your team. Include notes on both text *and* graphics.

Slide #1:

Slide #2:

Slide #3:

Slide #4:

Slide #5:

Slide #6:

Slide #7:

Slide #8:

Slide #9:

Slide #10:

Slide #11:

Slide #12:

Slide #13:

Slide #14:

Slide #15

C. Write a sentence using each of the rhetorical appeals to state your case. For example, writing a sentence with a logos-based appeal with have a rationale argument with plenty of facts and figures, an ethos-based appeal with include an appeal to ethics and/or expert testimony or authority figures, and a pathos-based appeal will include words with highly-charged emotional associations.

1. Logos:

2. Pathos:

3. Ethos:

CONCLUSION

Once you've done everything possible to ensure the precision and clarity of the message, you have to release your message into the world and have faith that it will be understood. Writing is a process, a journey, and an exploration. But the best writers also know how enough about their craft to get out of their own way. As W. Somerset Maugham once said, "The best style is the style you don't notice."

Happy Writing!

End

RESOURCES

Here are some resources that will help you continue improving your writing:

1. For grammar, structure, punctuation, and format, check out:

The Purdue University On-Line Writing Lab (OWL):

https://owl.english.purdue.edu/owl/

2. To perfect **MLA** formatting, check out:

The Modern Language Association (MLA):

www.mla.org

3. If your organization prefers the **APA** format, check out:

The American Psychological Association (APA):

www.apa.org

4. For more information on what **Tricarico Consulting** can offer you, visit our website:

www.tricaricoconsulting.com

ACKNOWLEDGMENTS

I would like to thank the following people for their help and support in making this publication possible:

- My wife and daughters
- The entire English Department at West Hills High School and all my students
- John Holler, who was always willing to discuss any scheme with me, no matter how crazy
- Laura Preble
- Lara Zielin
- My English and writing teachers, including Paula Skirfvars, Robin Luby, Kay Adams, Suzanne Geba, Geoffrey Anderson, Danelle Barton, Jane Schaffer, and Anne Foster. Many, most, or all of these lessons I learned from you first.

Thank you.

Dan

NOTES

NOTES

NOTES

NOTES

www.ingramcontent.com/pod-product-compliance
Lightning Source LLC
Chambersburg PA
CBHW020930180526
45163CB00007B/2963